Optimism

Optimism

Peter Dabbene

Copyright 2009 Peter Dabbene

ISBN 978-0-578-04116-2

Library of Congress Control Number: 2010900005

Dedicated with sincere thanks to all of the photographers who have allowed their work to be used in this volume.

TABLE OF CONTENTS

INTRODUCTION TO OPTIMISM	1
EXTINCT	2
NOTES FOR A STORY NEVER WRITTEN	4
COLERIDGE, AWAKE (THE MEMORY OF DREAMS)	6
ON THROWING OUT OLD FURNITURE	8
THE GRAPE THIEVES	10
NERO IS ALIVE	12
ADVICE FROM MY COMPUTER (ACTUAL JUNK E-MAIL SUBJECT HEADINGS)	13
KRYPTONIAN TRIPTYCH	16
DAYS WITHOUT WATCHES	18
BROOKLYN	20
CENTRAL AIR CONDITIONING AND CLIMATE CONTROL	21
THE DARK MATTER	22
RABBIT INTO DOG	24
HUDDLED 'ROUND THE HEARTH-LIGHT	26
FOURTH OF JULY, FIREFLY	27
SEX ON THE BEACH	30
TRAPPED IN AMBER	32
MONUMENT	34
FALSE IDYLL	36
(WRITING) MATHEMATICS	38
AFTER THE PARTY	39
ANTIFREEZE	40
WALKING, SUMMER, 3 A.M.	42
FEBRUARY EVENING	44
SHH	46
GRANDMOTHER, ASLEEP	48
FIELD	50
ANNULMENT	52
WEEKEND WARRIORS	54
WAITING TO LAUGH AT THE MOVIE TRAILER JOKE	56
OUT OF THE MOVIE-HOUSE	56

DREAMING UNDER A FULL MOON (DECEMBER 26, 2004)	58
TIME CAPSULES (THE SECRET FUNCTION OF BOOKS)	60
SNAKE (or SSS)	61
STONEHENGE	64
PHOTOS FOR SALE	66
PLUTONIAN ELEGY	68
A MASS OF CONTRADICTIONS	70
NO MORE BLACK SOCKS	72
SPRING, RESURGENT, RESPLENDENT	74
ODE TO PHILIP GLASS	75
COMET	78
A DREAM	80
SEARCHING FOR A HEARTBEAT	82
REFLECTION	84
TEETHING	85
A LATE NIGHT VISIT	86
VOYEUR	88
DÉJÀ VU	90
READING BY FLASHLIGHT	91
SPREADING MEMES IS FREE	92
ACKNOWLEDGEMENTS	93
PHOTO CREDITS	94
ABOUT THE AUTHOR	96

INTRODUCTION TO OPTIMISM

Modern poetry today is an increasingly hard sell. Like an outrageously-dressed teenager, it rarely gets noticed for itself, only for its trappings. These days a poet must enter the poetic arena through the back door, as it were. It helps to be a celebrity in some other field, of course, often one that has nothing to do with writing at all. It also helps to be young and ethnic, which works particularly well at poetry slams, or to write political poetry, or socially-conscious poetry in the inspirational, politically correct mode. One can also try stylistic tricks with the text itself to attract attention in the manner of the currently-in-vogue "visual poetry". And then there is the time-honored tradition of taking writing that is basically prose and using more-or-less clever line breaks to make it appear to be poetry. Nowhere today, it seems, is there room for, to paraphrase Wordsworth, emotions recollected in tranquility.

I know. I have edited a literary magazine for several years, and the quality of the majority of the poetry submissions I receive is, to put it nicely, not good. This is why I was so gratified a few years ago to receive a poetry submission from Peter Dabbene. You see, Peter's poetry has none of the attributes mentioned in the first paragraph. For the most part, it is simple, honest, and direct. It has a lyrical rhythm that, while graceful, is never pretentious. So, needless to say, I was thrilled when he asked me to write an introduction to his very fine poetry collection "Optimism". These fifty-one poems do precisely what good poetry should do: communicate the thoughts and feelings, observations, contents and discontents of the poet to the reader in the direct, simple but elegant manner that mere prose is unable to accomplish.

If you are a fan of true, unpretentious, contemporary poetry which, though personal in origin, has general appeal, this book is very much worth your attention.

Michael Matheny
Senior Editor
Cantarabooks/Cantaraville

EXTINCT

I would not feel threatened but for their sake

Blonde hair and blue eyes, killed by weak genes, now found only in kits and foreigners
Rotary dial telephones, holed up in old houses like fugitives and shut-ins
Saturday morning cartoons, victims of bloodless coups by political roundtables

What I would give to feel again
the thrill of exploring
VHF and UHF
     exotic and mysteriously static
Watching ghosts suffer poor reception
the last throes of the dying

These are animals which leave no fossils
Along with dodo, auk, and passenger pigeon,
consumed and digested
they have gone the way of the cursive Q,
The Lost Plays of Sophocles, the identity of Prussia:
Whispers from history books
     riding on telegraph rails

NOTES FOR A STORY NEVER WRITTEN

Talk about ____
Get into ____
Hint at ____, but don't get too specific

Do all these things, and wrap it up
In a distinctive style that's enjoyable to read
Make it the right length, neither too long nor too
                Short

Be profound/Make people think
But be entertaining/Leave them wanting more

Write for your audience/Write for yourself
Mix up the vocabulary/Keep it simple, stupid

Write what you know/But don't wallow in your past
Free your imagination/But ground it in reality

(Note: Work in sex, friendship, loyalty, work, love, disappointment, regret, and joy)

Got all that?
Then what are you waiting for?
(Burn this message)

COLERIDGE, AWAKE (THE MEMORY OF DREAMS)

Coleridge, awake!
in the narrow slits of time between dreaming and awareness
Quills lay strewn, scattered
Ink on floor, spattered
Images run to hide

The knock at the door
A man from Porlock, happy in forgetfulness
He sleeps to rest
I sleep to dream

I was conduit to an unfettered world inside me,
now dissipated into nothingness
Replaced by the hard, the real
The pens, the pencils
The images, tricking at fringes
Like trying to catch the ocean in one's hands

A lament, then:
As I lie in darkness, trying to remember
"A vision in a dream, a fragment"—
at least Coleridge returned with something

STEVE POLITI

friend was ready to start busting up the furniture.

"You get angry at somebody!" Chaney yelled into the phone, and all C. Vivian Stringer could do was listen.

"You drag your coaches into another room and you just raise hell!" he demanded. "And after that, you come down like an army thinkable loss to Tennessee, maybe the worst Stringer had ever endured. Chaney, a father figure and a friend, wanted Stringer to knock heads. He found out later that she already had.

She tried yelling. She tried cheering, team meetings and every psychological trick in the "One of the most?" Stringer said recently. "I would rank this as *the* most difficult."

But knowing the arc of her career, knowing how the highs have often followed the deepest lows, would anyone be surprised if this 19-12 season had a much more glamorous second act coming this month?

stark contrast to this fall when the Scarlet Knights were ranked second in the nation and expected to compete for their first NCAA title.

This month is about redemption for Stringer, about proving that the struggles bringing this team together for much of the

[See **POLITI**, Page 30]

A STARK REALITY AT XANADU

ON THROWING OUT OLD FURNITURE

Waiting to be picked up like orphans hoping for new life

The clear blue sky promises a better future

Surely someone wants these remnants? Surely someone cares?

I watch from the window, a voyeur

A few curious passers-by investigate

But find the remnants not to their liking

Perhaps they can sense the invisible weights attached

See the memories trapped in fibers

Maybe it scares them

Or maybe they have their own old furniture at home

Cigarette smoke from a dozen different brands

Liquid spills, stains that spark memories with just a glance

Torn holes where the puppies cut their teeth

Scratches on the edges where the cats manicured their claws

Sturdy constructions, solidly built by man

No other hand but man's will tear it down

The truck arrives, and the men show no emotion

Going about the job with the cool professionalism of a death squad

They pick up the items, one by one

Throw them into the gaping maw of the truck

How do they fit all that in there? I wonder

The answer comes in a sound that makes it hard to breathe

Like bones cracking, the legs are broken

Pillows vanish like kidnapped children

Dispatched

The mouth closes, the truck continues on its way

We are left behind, alone, reliant

On our memories for our memories

Which surely cannot last

THE GRAPE THIEVES

The grape-thieves hide their hair behind black shawl
and babushka, still two days till dye day.
Giddy and bloated with the fleeting wealth
of full shopping baskets, they discover
the succulent green orbs, too tempting to
resist. Lit by wary glances, practiced
fingers find their prey, twisting stems with no
great effort, like assassins snapping necks.

Secretly, in silence now, casually
bringing hand to mouth as if covering
a cough, or suddenly remembering,
or scratching an itch that can't be subdued,
the grapes pop into their mouths like pills, gummed
and swallowed to calm some inner turmoil.
The fruit fills their emptiness slowly, one
by one, like pebbles in a jar. Then, like
addicts, their shoulders relax once the deed
is done; all evidence has been destroyed.

Well-disguised caricatures of want, they
walk freely amid abundance in a
cavernous cornucopia, so full
and so vacant. The compulsion, passed
on by experience, to take what is
given—"Pride is the luxury of rich
and spoiled women"—isn't that what they'd say?

Embarrassed by the sight of shadow selves
and afraid of boldness, of rule-breaking,
of aged anarchists, the workers look
the other way as the grape-thieves move past,
bitter and unsatisfied, but at least
conscious of their failures. If they hear the
tisking or see bare, dark-haired heads shaking
in disgust, they give no indication.

NERO IS ALIVE

Nero is still alive

I see his signature on the walls of urban centers everywhere

In stylized splotches of black and red

Marking his presence among their decay

He is fiddling while they burn

ADVICE FROM MY COMPUTER (ACTUAL JUNK E-MAIL SUBJECT HEADINGS)

Just some advice…
What could be better?
Loneliness
Spotlighting
Daemonic
Roadsweepers
What would an MBA do for your career?
What would the words "university graduate" do for you?
Never put off until tomorrow what you can do today
Announcement
Congratulations
Find serenity
Looking for this?
Is smoking killing you?
Where would you like to go?
Change your love life forever
Wow Free Airline tickets!
Get the credit you deserve
I know you are bad
Eliminate your bills the Christian way
Would you like to…
Feel better - clean your colon
Quit smoking – free sample
Don't waste your money
Afraid of sex?
You'll be a sex machine
Haste makes waste
Joe said you needed to see this
The us government owes you money
Our government regularly gives away money in the form of
Xanax Available now
Xanax no doctor needed
Xanax now here
For the Person Who has Everything
Xanax
Every morning when I wake up…………
Xanax

Hottest toy of the year!

Xanax

Out of Xanax

Valium now in the product line

Free shipping on Valium

Buy Valium Cheap

Please give us some feedback

We Need Your Feedback

Looking for this?

Valium online

Here it is: your Phentermine

Prozac

Zoloft

The journey of a thousand miles begins with a single

Howdy

Want to travel for free?

Stop thinking about it and do it!

Check Now – you have water damage

Time is a great healer

Returned E-mail: User Unknown

Results in due time…

KRYPTONIAN TRIPTYCH

Fumbling excuses
Steel eyes behind plastic frames
Of course we all knew

Thinking of Krypton
He asks us what it feels like
To be truly home

A girl clips photos
Thinking how hopeless a world
If he wasn't real?

DAYS WITHOUT WATCHES

Hiding from the mailman but desperate for the mail
in a curtain-darkened room, I keep my neighborhood watches.
Wary of unscheduled disturbances, this house
is governed by the ticking of wall clocks, lit by artificial lights
while unsung melodies of birds collect at the window.
I have forgotten how to sing my song.

It sits in a dusty cardboard box, my song:
A 78, I remember: it came in the mail
years ago, when I sat at a different window.
There was a crazy old man who fixed watches
then, always telling us about strange lights
in the sky. He lived in a dilapidated old house.

I wonder: Do people talk about my house?
A place where you'll never hear a song;
the one holdout from Christmas lights,
containing the man who only communicates by mail.
And when we walk by, he just sits inside and watches,
crouched behind his covered window.

If eyes are the windows of the soul, I suppose a window
must be the eyes of its house
and of the man within it, who looks out that window and watches
for the mailman, who might one day bring a song
of blues, of melancholy, and when it arrives in the mail
maybe I'll finally put up those Christmas lights.

People will come from miles around to see those lights;
framing the door, illuminating the window—
I think you can order lights through the mail.
Anything can be delivered to your house
unless it's already there, sitting in a box under a bed, like my song,
packed away along with all my old watches.

I keep clocks, so they're not much needed, those watches.
Some were gold, some silver, some had press-button lights;
I would've liked a watch that played a little song.
My favorite had a slight crack in its face, like my window.

Still, watches are for outside the house
and why leave home, when you've got the mail?

I'm happy enough, I think—stalking the mail, passing days without watches.
I have clocks in my house, and dimmed lights
and a cracked window that sings my song.

BROOKLYN

When you left

it was like the Dodgers leaving Brooklyn

a stadium emptied out

a home destroyed

they moved to California to start again

like everyone does

even you

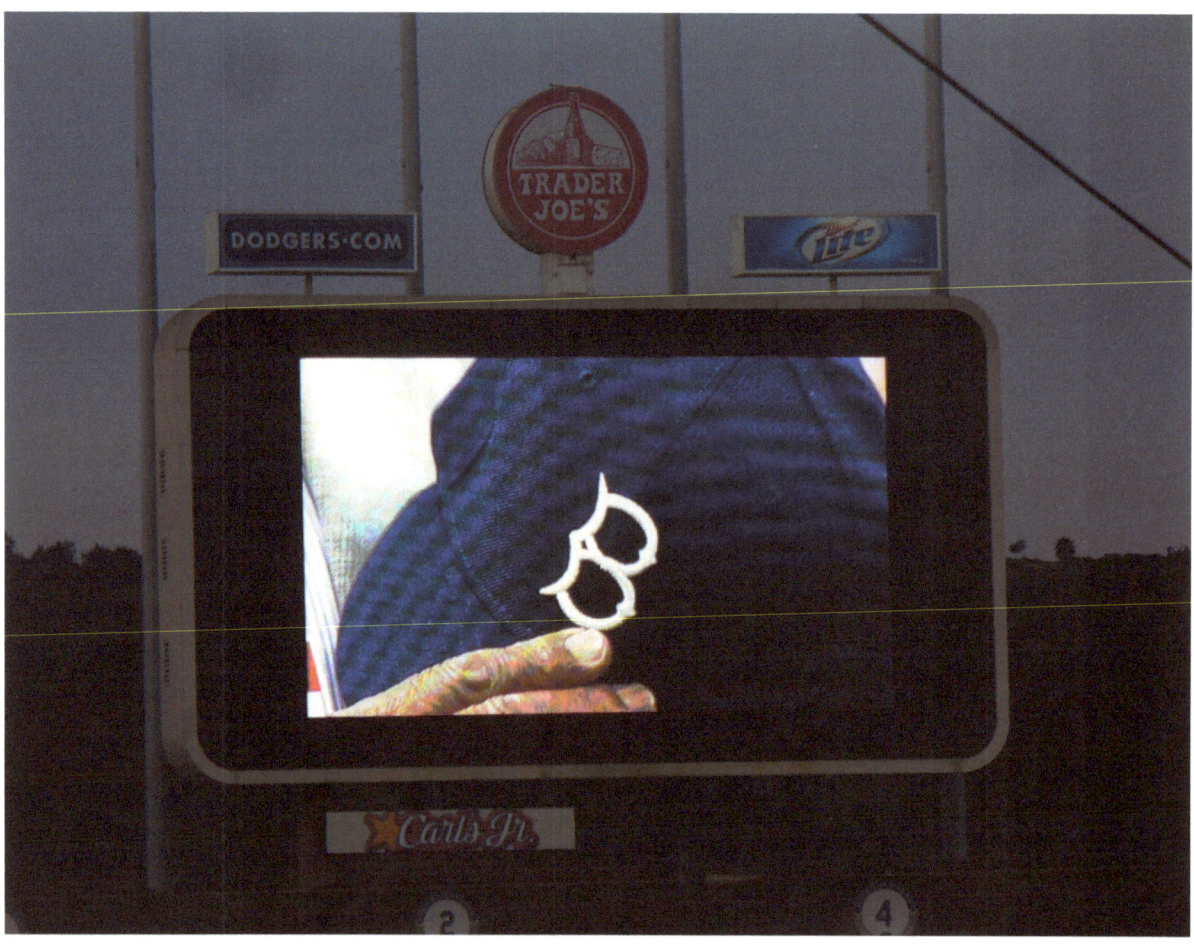

CENTRAL AIR CONDITIONING AND CLIMATE CONTROL

And so we sit, locked inside our perfect world

Windows sealed up tight

No longer the comforting drone of window-mounted air conditioners

Or the soft whipping of fans cutting a summer breeze down to size

The regulated lament of the seasons

I like to watch the seasons change from inside my window pane

Me, I've got my slice of heaven

My indoor air's at 67.

THE DARK MATTER

Detectable only by the measure of its absence
Something missing, undocumented
Filling the space between us
Is it what keeps us together?
What forces us apart?
We two:
      a steady star, shining beacon to the loveless
      an asteroid, caroming through space on an uncharted course
      attracted

Twin telescopes, enhancing limited eyesight
Are not enough to see what drives us
To know the tantalizing, distant knowable
Peering past our eyes
Into an invisible world of mysterious motivations
Where science fails us

Clutching your hand tight, it seems
There can't be anything more than this
But there is—
We calculate the distance between us
And know that something's unaccounted for

Unseen, this weight between you and me
    (not gravity)
Makes up most of our existence
Our modest secrets become
A vast expanse, expanding
Our galaxies drifting apart
The gravity grows heavier
But our hold on each other is weakening

What keeps us together, then
When most of our universe
Is dark matter?

RABBIT INTO DOG

As shocked as her prey,
I watch
This warm, gentle dog
Clutching a baby rabbit in her jaws

Is this how mothers in court feel when,
In the face of damning evidence,
They scream that their baby is not a killer?

This is not hard little pellets of processed who-knows-what
Or biscuits specially coated to prevent plaque
On her savage teeth
The canine's canines

The rabbit's eyes offer acceptance
The order of things, and all
National Geographic come to life, three feet away
I thought we were removed from this
As far removed as the nearest slaughterhouse
Rabbit disappears into dog
We continue on our walk

HUDDLED 'ROUND THE HEARTH-LIGHT

I remember how we huddled
'round the cable box at night
For warmth
Safe in its dull buzz-hum
We'd gather before the hearth-light
The soft glow of the television
We were cast in shades of blue-white
As it lit the darkness, throwing lightning storms
Illuminating as it obscured us

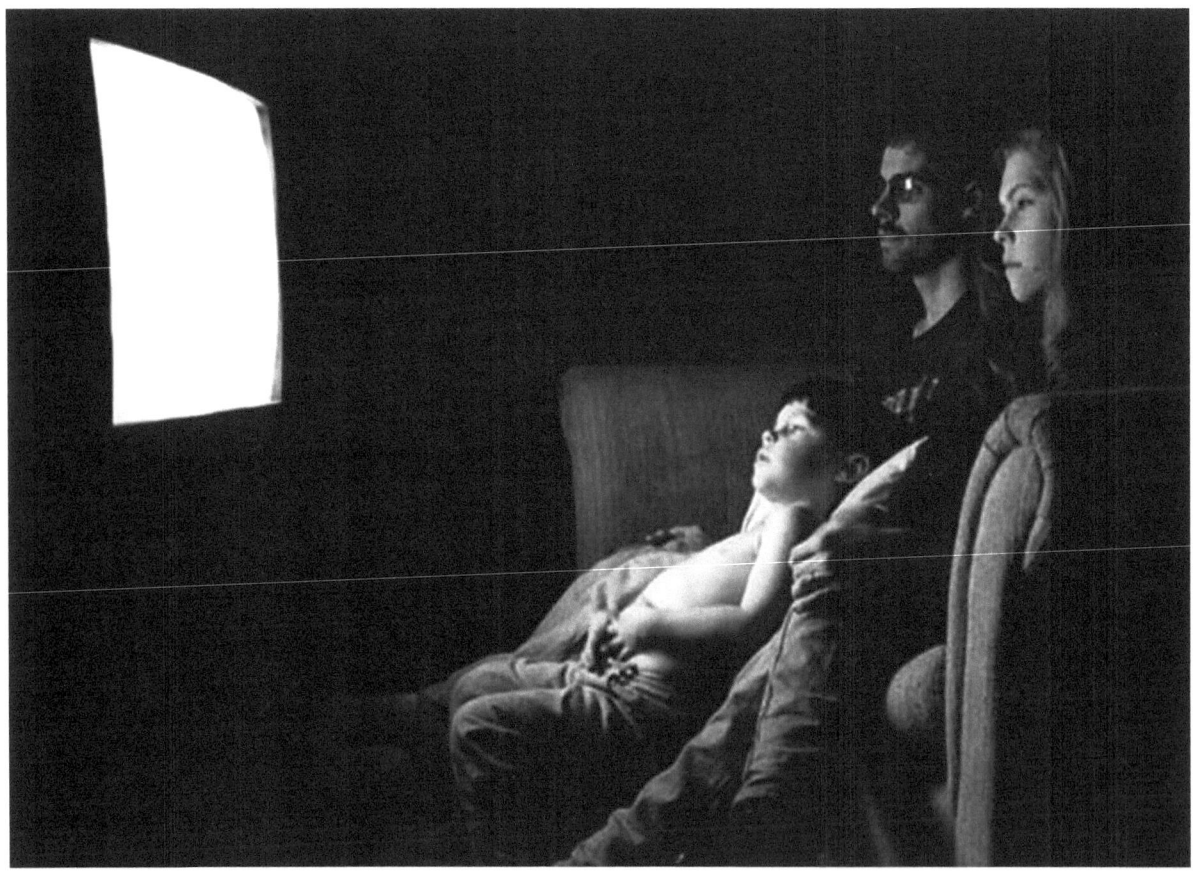

FOURTH OF JULY, FIREFLY

Those poor people
West of the Rockies, they have never seen this
I have never seen the Grand Canyon, but they have never seen this
Stars in the sky, fireflies in the trees below,
And me, bathed in the sticky warmth of their illuminations

Catching them seems natural
Gentle motions, like Tai Chi
They alight on a slowly swinging arm (my palm upraised)
A smooth twist of the wrist and they're looking at the world through glass

An early evening lit by lightning bugs,
Collected in a jar
A night to steal your loneliness away
From crowds of expectant patriots

The neighbors emerge from their hiding-houses
Our skin prickles in the imminent night air

As the sky fades from blue to black,
Let us take
A moment's pause to repel mosquitoes
Carrying the latest horrible disease

At seven lightning bugs, I stop
Seven seems a good number for companionship
All the in-lightning I'll need
Come see where I live, firefly

Inside the house, I carry my jar like a talisman
Guiding me in darkness unsullied by electric light
The bugs flash faster,
Seeing a kindred spirit in the blinking light of the answering machine
(Messages await, the bugs look for mates)
They will go unanswered

Sit down on the couch, open up the shades
The sky begins to skyrocket with explosions and colors
Fading out after only a brief moment in this universe
Then back to ashes

Shine the brightest light, make the loudest noise
Ephemeral is not a word for nations born of revolution

Fireflies in a jar flash with rhythmic syncopation
Stray fireworks linger with the stars
But they cannot hold on forever
They are dismissed
Subjects of a transitory genus
Living their short bug lives

Glowing, burning briefly in the sky
Up in smoke like so many ill considered plans
Leaving ghost marks on our canopy

When the stars have re-emerged, fireflies again catch the eye
There are seven in my jar
They don't think about where they're going
It's all instinct; they can't be stopped

I lift the lid, shake their clear cage
And off they fly to burn themselves up
A few seconds later I see them in the trees and grass
Blinking high and low
The pulse of life
All they can do is light up the darkness for a few seconds

Bye bye, firefly
Happy Fourth of July

SEX ON THE BEACH

In dim, indoor light
She shakes off winter and approaches the bar
Waits for the bartender, restless, her hands sliding along wooden edges dull with wear
Sits, her coat draped over one knee in a way that's got to mean something
One foot poised on the bronze foot rail; she's ready

Eyes scanning the room, she pulls out a cigarette
No lighters offered, she does it herself
The men here are busy being absorbed into big screen TVs
Watching sports, movies—fantasies
While she sits alone,
Too real, too much commitment, too much baggage

I focus on her lips, pale pink from the cold
They ask for "Sex on the Beach"
She sits and stares at nothing
She wants to feel something, anything;
Be somewhere else, with someone—anyone?
She runs a finger through lingering water rings of drinks long gone
Her breasts betray a little sigh

Vodka, orange juice, cranberry, pineapple
A bit of the hard stuff with an exotic tang
Strange colors in these shadows
From liquid sunshine in a fancy glass

What would she look like in a swimsuit?
At night, looking up at stars
Her skin, glowing red from a day on the sand
Her body, radiating captured heat
The breeze bringing the smell of salt, and her
Charged libido from the fresh air and sun and sea
Elements, elemental, raw, like fucking
There, and here, a fantasy, in person
Alone, at a bar, with a drink

TRAPPED IN AMBER

Somewhere between an empty beer bottle
And a girl I once knew…
This intersection, curve hidden, threatening collision

Stopped, at a flashing yellow light
Unsure whether to stay or go
Frozen like insect in amber

Amber glow, not yellow like modern traffic lights
Amber like aged pictures
Like yellowed fingernails

Tree-lined streets, darkened sky,
Remembering other places, other times
Amber, like her hair, like her name

Trapped between brown and yellow
Idling in neutral while a signal
Flashes life before my eyes

Trapped at a crossroads
Bathed in amber and unable to move
Proceed with caution—at the risk of going nowhere

MONUMENT

Monument on the side of the road;
traffic passes it by
words engraved, worn down by time
paid no attention
weeds choke its meaning

A chance stop brings me to
Its wisdom from another age

She sits in her wheelchair
rooted to the past
credo into epitaph
ignored and obsolete
giving up the right to fight

erosion takes its toll

FALSE IDYLL

The garden, like Eden, overgrown and fruitful, higher than my head
It took days to traverse in my child's mind, like a trek through densest African jungles
Plump grapes littered the narrow paths
And in the center of the living labyrinth, the dogs
Protectors and protected (Minotaur, and Cerberus, both)
And them, he smiling with cigar
She hunched and all a-fuss
Their voices croaking, creaking

This is my memory
Like the vegetables, shrunken and desiccated
Not looming so large in my mind
Anymore
There's no room for it, as there was then
Leaching out the last bits, like juice from strawberries
Jot it down before it disappears

Halcyon days have come and gone
Withered vines and empty cages are all I can find
Mountains of coal, down to hills, down to piles
A deficiency of memory perception
Loss, calibrated for reality
Still looking for that memory
Memories can lie, they say
This is my thatwhat
Lost in my sincewhen

(WRITING) MATHEMATICS

Twelve hundred fifty words thought per minute, on average;
Two hundred fifty spoken, at full speed;
Sixty typed, if you've taken a class;
And now, a mystery, please pay heed:

Where, oh where, do the lost words go?
What will they look like, if they ever show?
Have they been spun into memory from tangled weaves of thought?
Are they sitting in stomachs, tied into knots?

The gap grows greater each passing day
Bits of thoughts and dialogue frittered away;
To our words, our selves, let us say goodbye
A prelude to mortality, as they fade and die.

AFTER THE PARTY

When everyone has gone, or gone to sleep,
I sit alone, in a still house
It is not the alcohol that hurts
But surveying the damage—
The connections teased, then severed
Clean the plates, clean the cups
Drain the drink down the sink
Until it looks like no one ever came
And all that's left are fuzzy memories

ANTIFREEZE

Playing the waiting game
A trail of antifreeze
marks my entry
A smoking Olds Cutlass Supreme
Unpainted
A silent dead steaming hulk
Joyce Kilmer has saved me from the fire
Now it exacts its price for salvation;
sitting in a dead car,
I turn at every sound
in the sparsely inhabited parking lot
A Chevy stares ----
Waiting watching
as the temperature gauge
lowly slowly ticks down from 260 degrees;
A place of sanctuary with its mask removed
2 a.m. on a Thursday
A haunted, deserted shell
Here, life is not meant for more than 5 minutes at a time
Then shuttle off to the next number on the road
This place feels like wandering
No destination but the endless stream of rest areas, differentiated
only
by the spelling of anonymous names

<u>tick, tick, tick</u>

the temperature drops oh so slowly, lowly
I don't have the guts to sleep here
Scanning vacation pamphlets by dim, distant light
Trying to decide where to wish I was
Making the most of this meantime
I'm tired
I want to go home
tick,tick,tick

WALKING, SUMMER, 3 A.M.

Walking
for some hours
in between the
college students
returning from
wherever they go
at night
and the
paper deliverers
who cannot afford
the time to walk their routes

is quiet
and peace

Motion sensors are alarmed at my presence
They are poised to illuminate
Anything bigger than a rabbit

I am bigger than a rabbit

Exposure in harsh artificial light
       jarring
then soothing—illuminating the fact
that no one else is here
just traces of people, like footprints
   or ancient books

They lie inside sleeping, the faceless
Never to emerge for all I know, their cars left behind
Metal monuments to those who have gone away

The sun marks the end of my etude on solitude
Watching the dawn break
Over houses that have begun to light up
One bathroom at a time
They call this the beginning but I know the truth
The best part of the day is past
And everything else is coda, epitaph

FEBRUARY EVENING

the crowd of teens with bats
emerging from the park
on a strangely warm and placid February evening
and all I can think about is
who they're going after
and why
how I would defend myself
if they turned on me
daydreams of heroic actions
the beginnings of an adrenaline rush
delusions of grandeur and invincibility
fight a fear of actually becoming involved
all of everything...

falls apart
amid the eavesdropping
of youths discussing their heroes
who carry bats
and use them...

to play baseball

SHH

Establish
Furnish
Burnish
Distinguish
Polish
Nourish
Tarnish
Languish
Anguish
Demolish
Refurbish
Finish
Publish
Flourish
Relish
Perish
Vanish

GRANDMOTHER, ASLEEP

Asleep, all equal in fantasy selves
Age disappears
Dreaming ourselves young

Now her fantasies come during the day, unwelcome
Escaped from their century prison

She sleeps the sleep of the exhausted
Of the mother, and of the father
Of the brittle bone weary
Of the wrinkled skin parched
She sleeps the sleep of the dead, dreamless

FIELD

They proceed in rigid rows, coaxing order from nature,
bending regularly to examine the dirt,
like blue-jacketed jays mining for worms.
Their squawks and cackles come at odd moments
on high frequencies, interrupting the cicadas' summer singing.

With shovels and backhoes, they push, they prod, they plead
for the field to give up its secrets.

The day passes slowly, and they comb the field
with increasing absentness,
some lingering too long as if silently called to stay.
As the sun squints its final glances, they gather in their yellow tape;
the invasion is over, trespassers soon to be gone.

Behind high grass
hidden, lies a body.

It will consume its secrets, forgetting what came before
and once again the field will be deserted,
left to rest in peace.

ANNULMENT

Freeze it all in motion, now blink it all away,
Excusing our sorrows and pardoning our sins
No one's to blame, for it never took place
Amnesiacs who still remember
Expunge the records
We
    are
        clean
            again.

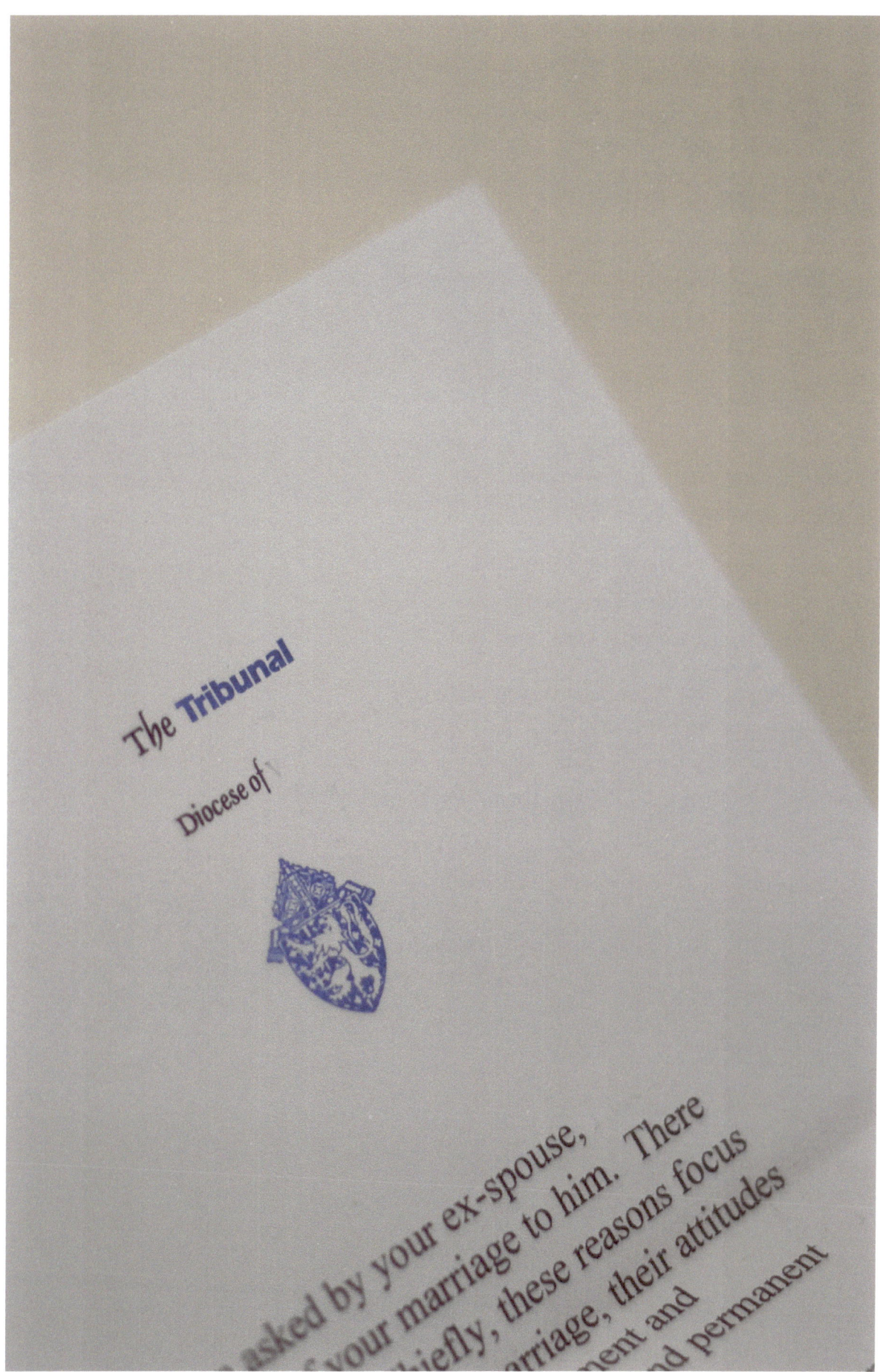

WEEKEND WARRIORS

They arrive one by one, out of SUVs
and Minivans parked in formation,
clutching bottles of water and bright fluorescent tonics,
stretching petrified limbs in concession to age
while others go without — to play "cold," this is living on the edge.
Conversation flows, punctuated with child-rearing tips and gossip
until, armor-clad in knee braces and ankle guards,
daubing sunscreen like war paint,
their faces change.

Gripping the ball, they push themselves;
grunting exertions, drowning the week's frustrations
in testosterone and sweat

Craving minds free of worried thought,
now filled only with instant, ingrained response,
everything falls away but comrades, and competition

Tribes tasting bitter defeat, choked and swallowed whole
to rot in guts till next week;
Or victory to speed the struggles of family and work;
celebrated once aloud, savored many times in quiet reflection

All the while, strains and sprains
sore backs and shaky knees
remind them
they are
still
alive

WAITING TO LAUGH AT THE MOVIE TRAILER JOKE

Having seen this scene a dozen times
In commercials, we still laugh loudest
At the safe, prepared-for joke
Proving we're on cue
Familiarity breeds content

OUT OF THE MOVIE-HOUSE

Blinded and full of bluster we emerge
Glowing like junkies, pleasure-fixed and restless
Gods, not men, not boys, unchained, unleashed

DREAMING UNDER A FULL MOON (DECEMBER 26, 2004)

Lost on an Ocean of Storms, I foundered

Adrift off the Known Sea, I explored

Forgetting the Sea of Crises

Forgetting the Lake of Death

I fell into a Marsh of Sleep

And swam in a Lake of Dreams

TIME CAPSULES (THE SECRET FUNCTION OF BOOKS)

Lost and forgotten inside the covers of books, random items become

Seeds of memory, discarded like acorns on a forest floor

Tomes, serving as tombs, or rather, vaults

Withered hands cracking weathered spines, revealing marrow

Musty, dusty, and heavy with the weight of time

Notes, receipts, stray hairs, and stains

Now anchors to summon moments from before

Kept safely secret by obscure titles and subjects

With no curious borrowers disturbing

These memories grow steadily in silence

Pressed between pages, like autumn leaves preserved

SNAKE (or SSS)

Slandered serpent, libeled and
                       lowly, hiding
            in the
                   grass
       It is my
                    misfortune
                                 that
                                    your
                                        ancient
                                  mammal memories
                                    associate
                                  sibilance
                                      with
                                      the
                                    sinister
                                          My
                                            cousins,
                                      hiding in
                                          trees,
                                  swimming in
                                        seas,
                                      mind
                                  our business
                                  while,
                                we admit,
                               taking a
                             certain
                        pride
                         thinking
                     of children
                      at
                   petting
                zoos
                 scared to
                 touch,
               and
               don't
                    say
                        you
                            don't

turn
on the hiss
of a tire
leaking air,
or
squirm
at
the
thought of
a snake
squeezing
into
bed,
or
feel a twinge and
shudder
when you
see
me
adjacent to
an apple.
All
animals move
but
only
one
slithers
so
at least
I'm
unique,
even if
I can't
use
scissors

STONEHENGE

STONEHENGE

PAPERWEIGHT

POSTCARD   K   3
   P   A   E   D   FRISBEE
   E   S   Y   P   M   P
   N   H   C   U   A   O
   D   T   H   Z   G   S
   A   R   A   Z   N   T
   N   A   I   L   E   E
   T   Y   N   E   T   R

HAT

I own it now.

PHOTOS FOR SALE

We search through the photos for a life worth co-opting
It sounds bad, I know, but don't worry – they're not using them
The quarter bowl bears a few treasures – a man at the Wailing Wall, smiling;
We see photos of couples – victims of bad break-ups?
A young man's high school graduation photo – why is that here?
"Maybe he didn't like the way he looked in that picture."
"Too vain or insecure, the way high schoolers are."
"Maybe he's a disappeared drug addict the family just wants to forget."
"Maybe he was killed by a drunk driver and it hurts too much to remember."
They hate to remember, they long to forget
These photos of dead lives and living dead
We'll take those cast-offs;
They'll live in our minds.

The larger photos are more expensive, some almost a dollar
Professional wedding-day portraits, vintage army IDs, and more
For every experience, a buyer; for every photo, a seller
I look in my wallet and find a few shots of my wife, my children
They're small (wallet-size), only worth a quarter in this tragic marketplace
What a bargain!
I remove them and place them in the bowl;
Seeing them staring back from behind wall-mounted fishbowls relaxes me.
Dennis has come prepared:
He's cut a sheet of twelve unused kindergarten graduation photos
He drops them in
We each remove a picture from the bowl, making sure not to take our own.
Dennis has a picture of an older couple; this week he'll play the gentleman.
I get a picture of three college-aged girls on vacation somewhere sunny.
"Maybe they got into a fight, and aren't friends anymore."
"Over a guy, maybe."
"Or philosophical differences."
The eyes of the one on the right capture me immediately;
I put the photo in my wallet; for the week, I'll see the world from her eyes.
Next week we'll be back, to see if our lives had any takers
And pull new ones for ourselves from plastic fishbowls

67

PLUTONIAN ELEGY

Distanced far amid these heavenly bodies
Hides the wretched runt in our celestial litter
Death, and ferryman, lurking in dim, ancient light
Riding Neptune's riptides
Clinging in indifference to names bestowed, not earned

Redraw the maps
Rewrite the books
No longer will my very educated mother
Show us nine planets
Death and the ferryman do not care

Death and the ferryman have gazed, will gaze impassively

Long beyond our ability to classify
To compartmentalize
To subdivide
To organize

Out of reach

Our frozen flower

A sphere by any other name would
                              taste as cold

                              appear as small

                              seem as remote

                              linger as steadfastly

A MASS OF CONTRADICTIONS

Carrying the weight of years, a
Mass of contradictions appears
Bending to the task of impositions
Bearing institution's straitjackets

And the sickle child whines,
Having memorized his lines
Absorbing woody pew-stink
Running fingers along tongues, in grooves

Even while he's squirming,
This is all the while confirming
"I belong here, with you all"
Because where else is there to go?

Kneeling, sneaking glances through his glasses
At the rows ahead (the girls' forbidden asses)
Seeing only heavy heads on lolling necks
Anchored by generations of tradition

With the other boys he's lip-synching
When he smells that something's stinking
Wafting through the cavern,
Perfume clouds their shiny halos

Though he's sainting in the back row
Soon he's fainting in the back row,
A martyr to the cause
Of heavy incense in the air

Then it's time, and bells are ringing
Within moments, the choir's singing
Necco Wafers, Tiddly Winking, plates that catch 'em if they drop
Fingered food, solemn line-up, he just wants it all to stop

He's still kneeling, though he's swaying
But through it all he's staying
Staying, because where else is there to go
Except outside—

While everyone he knows is inside saying
"Amen" and after service, staying
To chat about that little boy
Who would not sit still in church

NO MORE BLACK SOCKS

Abandon black socks? I've *been* ready
I don't need cues to be responsible, or steady
Ubiquitous black socks – in winter, woolen, thick and heavy
In summer they're just thin, see-through, full of holes and sweaty

Once upon a time I wore my black socks proudly
Even in my off-hours they did my shouting loudly
On the street with shorts and sneakers, or driving in my Audi
I cared not at all that to some, I looked a little dowdy

Yes, I am that old man (but younger)
Who seems oblivious to fashionmongers
Or maybe, in my case, it's something stronger
Could those black socks feed a power hunger?

As a child I wore high white socks, curled tight against the calf
Socks so long they could have served their purpose cut in half
To wear them as a working man would have proved a monstrous gaffe
These were socks one never sees on a corporation's suited staff

Those childhood socks had stripes, in every color of the rainbow
I picked socks to suit my mood, the way wine lovers might choose Bordeaux
I wore red or orange stripes for sunny days, and black or gray for snow
But the last thing on my mind was appearing *apropos*

These days I match my socks with suits and ties that make my mood
I tread a sort of middle ground, clad in muted colors too subdued
To feel that joy of being young, to once again elude
The problems black socks bring; thus, at the risk of seeming crude:

No longer will I worry about when my pension's vested
Nor attend weddings whose invitations read "Black Tie Requested"
I'll donate all my suits (even my favorite double-breasted)
I won't compete with life, but let it move me, uncontested

"No more black socks," I tell you – this is me, restated
A good decision, I suppose, if a bit belated
I'll wear white socks with stripes, any time I feel it's rated
Or if the desire strikes me I'll go naked, as created

SPRING, RESURGENT, RESPLENDENT

First sprouts from limb trimmed trees

Proudly displaying their colors on thin, spindly branches

Like young girls presenting newly nail-polished fingers to nervous fathers

ODE TO PHILIP GLASS

This is an ode to Philip Glass

This is an ode to Philip Glass

This is an ode to Philip Glass

This is an ode to Philip Glass

This is an ode to Philip

                        Glass

This is an ode to Philip

                        Glass

This is an ode to

                        Philip Glass

This is an ode

An ode

An ode

Anode

Anode

Anode

Anode to Philip Glass

Anode to Philip Glass

Anode to PhilipGlass

Anode to PhilipGlass

THIS is an ode to Philip Glass

THIS IS AN ode to Philip GLASS

THIS IS AN ODE TO PHILIP GLASS

THIS IS AN ODE TO PHILIP GLASS

THIS IS AN ODE TO PHILIP GLASS

THISISANODETOPHILIPGLASSTHISISANODETOPHILIPGLASS

THIS IS AN ODE

                TO PHILIP Glass

Philip Glass

Philip Glass

Philip Glass

Philip Glass

Philip

Philip

Philip

    Glass

Philip Glass

Philip Glass this is

        an ode to

Philip Glass this is

        an ode to

Philip Glass this is

        an ode to

An ode to Philip Glass

This is an ode to Philip Glass

COMET

It harps and dances
Teases, taunts, and trances
Enhances glances to the sky
Lies just beyond our reach

Battling horizons
We take our hopes and fears on
Through the rip streaming forth the light
As the long dawn parades across the night

In the fields, we awe at such
That which we see but cannot touch

A DREAM

In my dream,
I am running

Alongside me is every dog we've ever owned
Their tongues flapping out the sides of their mouths
I watch them run, and smile
My private flock, my private stock of best friends
With no leashes and no fences

In my dream,
The backyard goes on forever;
Down a hill
Someone awaits

In my dream,
I am running to you. You,
Waiting
(With every cat we've ever owned)

Their purring rumbles through the quiet air
As they weave between your legs
Rub against your feet

In my dream, I am never winded
And we are never old
The weather is pleasantly warm
And the lemonade always cold

The grass is always green
In my slumber-scenes

I will be there soon
I am coming

SEARCHING FOR A HEARTBEAT

Like old men lingering
With metal detectors in the sand
Fighting the ocean's refrain
    Listening for signs of hidden treasure

We are living with suspicions but no proof
Except nausea, a sense that something's off
And a calendar, not always to be trusted
    So we have arrived:

    cold metal hovers
        over
  her warm and worried belly
      touches
  and we are silent

After long minutes listening,
Above amplified white noise
    Come his words of consolation:

"It's still early"
"Next time you'll hear it"

Then, one last try
Resigned, impatient –
    Rapid-fire heartbeat verifying everything

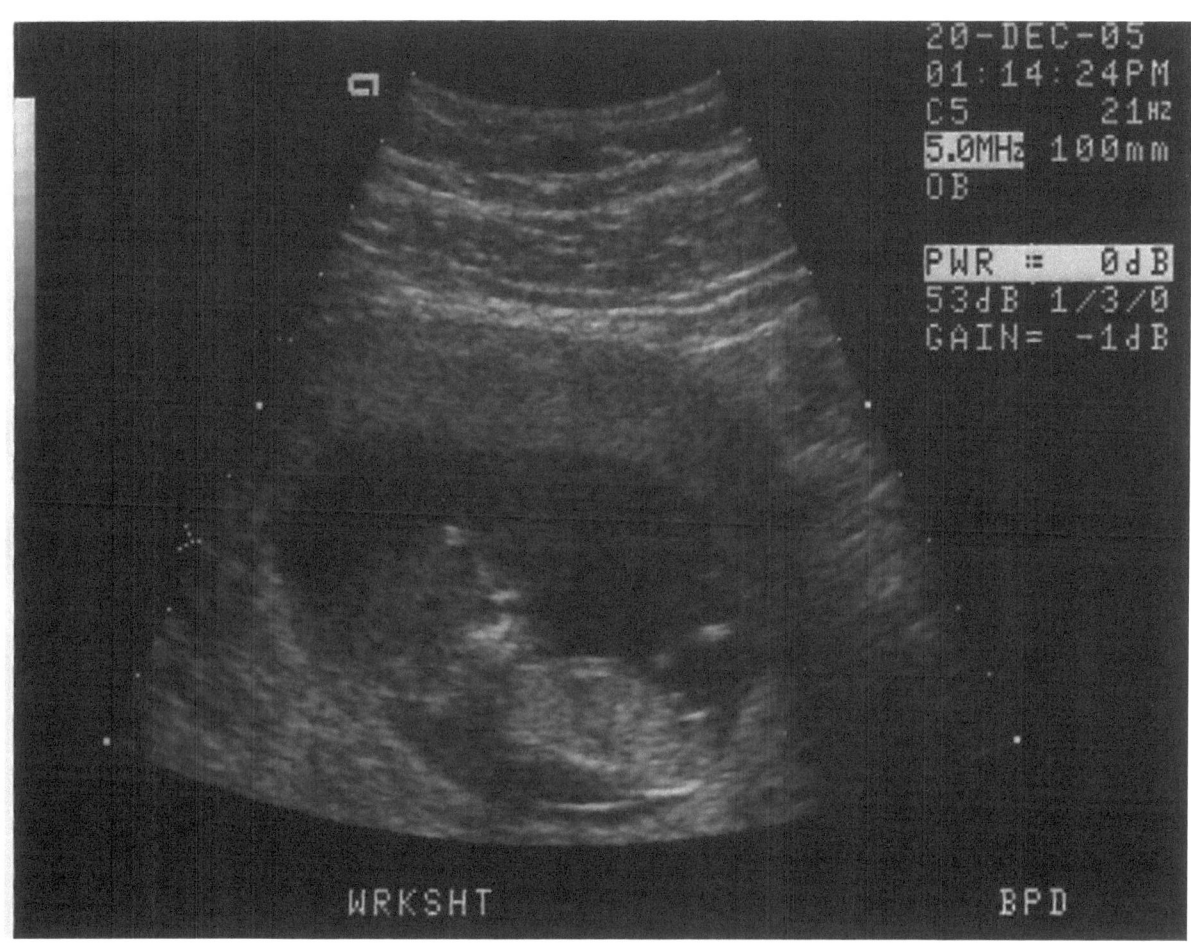

REFLECTION

An ancient tree reflected on a lake's shiny surface

the tree has grown

Twin cast into endless depths

disturbed only by the rain-drips

that ripple in this place

roots extending into branches

this is true reflection

roots extending into branches

my infant son's face,

his mother's eyes, his father's lips

left becomes right, right becomes left

familiar yet unknown,

An ancient tree reflected on a lake's shiny surface

TEETHING

So difficult to watch, helpless
as pearl-white nubs burrow through tender
gumlines, wreaking havoc, provoking tears

So difficult to whisper soothing tones
and promise assurances during this, the
first of many pains I cannot protect against

A LATE NIGHT VISIT

A crackle over the monitor spoils the still night air
Nervous and slit-eyed, she wakes and waits,
Lying and listening, ever the expectant mother
A low moan comes, followed by baby babble—
First questioning, then confident
He is finding his voice, they say

Creeping in, newly uncertain,
She sees dark eyes reflecting dim, hesitant light
Slowly revealed are a sturdy crib, tousled blankets
And a crooked smile, trusting and pure with delight,
Saying silently and succinctly:
"I knew you'd come"

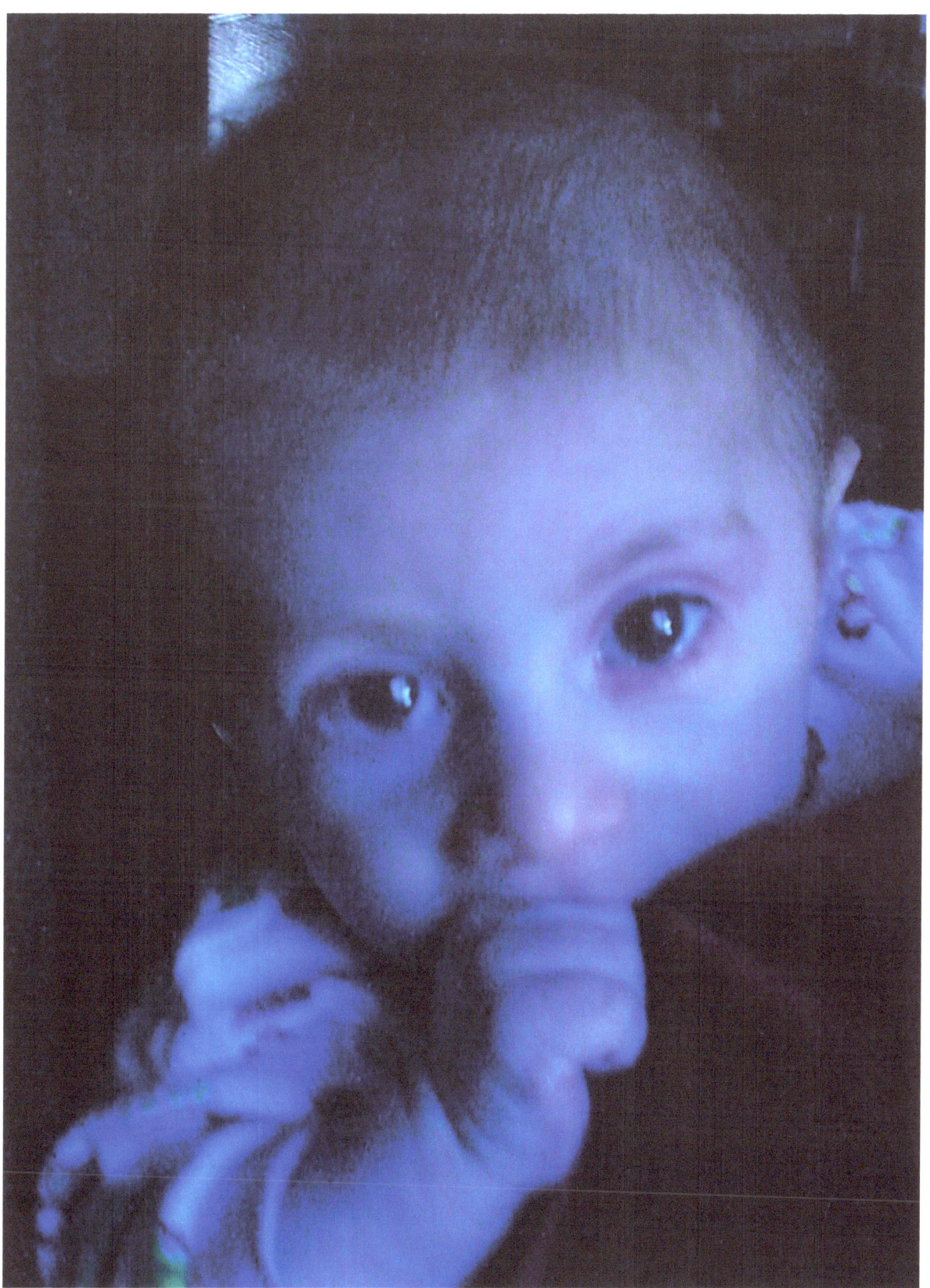

VOYEUR

Passive, I have become
An addict, eager for the next fix

In backyards and basement theaters
Experiencing everything the first time, again
Basking in reflected glories lessened
Wincing from mirrored pain curtailed
Your eyes replacing mine, lost to routine
First glances through second sight
Your eyes wide, absorbing images
Like cameras, as I stage-manage scenes

I live in margins, pushed to the edges of the chronicles of your life

Even television has lost its gilded luster
Except for watching you watching
Delighting when you grin at slapstick
Touched when you cry at maudlin melodrama

Everything seems simple
Watching a child learning limits

With you a buffer making sensation distant
I feel myself receding
Changing diapers and eating lotus-leaves
Suffering withdrawal when you sleep

Then, watching an independent streak develop,
It hits:
The knowledge that this can't last forever

Out of a fugue, awakened from a zombie-state
By the memory of a life before
My experience awakened through yours
Hearing in your ambitions the echoes of my own
Seeing them become clear again

On one road merged from two intertwined, we travel
Forging separate paths, together

DÉJÀ VU

These motions seem familiar, but blurred as in a dream

Lack of sleep making it that much more surreal

Will it be the same this time?

Probably not, he says,

Something about stepping in the same river twice

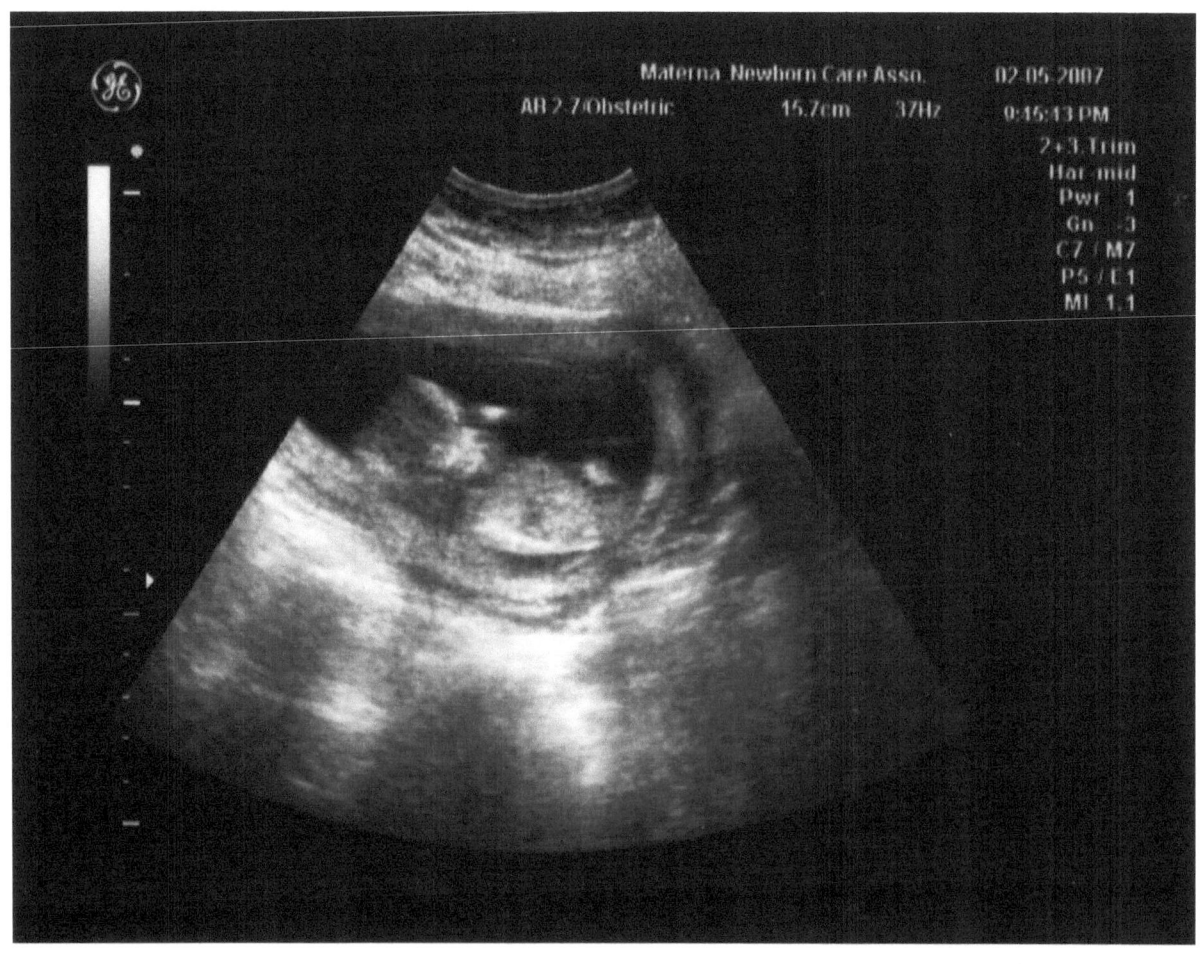

READING BY FLASHLIGHT

The pages luminesce, reflecting bright flashlight like diamonds
The words, in ragged rows upon the page, precious
They emerge to squinting eyes, the dull shine of coal
Mine, buried inside this mine, mining
Artificial underground, covered under blankets
In the middle of the night

In the dark, everyone is children
  even if
instead of parents' wrath
  I am still for spouse's sleeping;
instead of late night baseball, cheap radio pressed to ear
  the only noise mutters from her dreams

While she sleeps,
All we dreamers lay awake,
Bonded in our solitude

SPREADING MEMES IS FREE

I like to walk the streets humming or whistling an irritating tune
Once they hear it, they're infected; there's no way to avoid it
This is my equal playing field, this is my created equal
They cannot shut me up, so I take advantage
I explain to bystanders that the world is balanced on the back of all the petrified thoughts of dinosaurs
I tell them that rain is not really water until it comes into contact with something else
I warn them that bugs are plotting to overthrow humanity very soon, swarming and killing us
One person at a time

In their heads like radio songs
They can't pretend they never heard me
No matter what I say
And the next time they look at bugs, or the rain, or a picture of the Earth,
I will have made my mark.

ACKNOWLEDGEMENTS

The print and online journals that first published some of these poems:

"Nero Is Alive," "Huddled 'Round the Hearth-Light," "Comet," "Out of the Movie-House," and "False Idyll" were published online in Ampersand Poetry Journal (Autumn 2006)

"Comet" and "On Throwing Out Old Furniture" were published in California Quarterly Volume 32, Number 1 (Spring 2006)

"Shh" was published in Lady Churchill's Rosebud Wristlet (November 2005) and Bogg No. 73/74 (2006)

"Kryptonian Triptych," "The Grape Thieves," and "Waiting to Laugh at the Movie Trailer Joke" were published online in Hinge Online Volume 7:2 (August 2006)

"No More Black Socks" was published in Journal of New Jersey Poets Volume 31 (2006) and in The Griffin (2006)

"Spring, Resurgent, Resplendent" and "Ode to Philip Glass" were published in Zillah Volume 6, issue 1(Spring 2006)

"A Dream" was published online in Apple Valley Review Volume 1, Number 1 (Spring 2006)

"Spreading Memes Is Free" was published online in White Leaf Review Issue 4 (Spring 2006)

"Notes for a Story Never Written" was published in ByLine, June 2006

"Grandmother, Asleep" and "Rabbit into Dog" were published online in Adagio Verse Quarterly (2006)

"Monument" was published (as "Memento") in BluePrintReview #1 (2006)

"Searching for a Heartbeat" was published online in Red River Review, May 2007

"A Late Night Visit" was published online in Rokovoko, June 2007

"Trapped in Amber" was published in SLAB #2 (2007)

"Plutonian Elegy," "Brooklyn," "Weekend Warriors," "Field," and "Snake" were published in Cantaraville Three (April 2008)

"Plutonian Elegy" was published online in Astropoetica Volume 6.2 (Spring 2008)

"Extinct" was published online in Bread and Lightning (2008)

PHOTO CREDITS

"Half Full" (cover image) is used by permission of Brian Utesch (www.brianuteschphotography.com)

"Extinct" (page 3) is used by permission of Paul Speller (www.flickr.com/bitospud)

"One Day" (page 5) is used by permission of George E. Brown (www.georgebrownphotography.com)

"A Stark Reality at Xanadu" (page 7) is used by permission of Matthew P. Hintz

"Dumped" (page 9) is used by permission of James Caws (www.jamescaws.co.uk)

"2 Old Ladies" (page 11) is used by permission of Kip Hudson

"Nero – IFU ~ Graffiti on a Boxcar in Pico Rivera, CA 7-24-7" (page 12) is used by permission of Brian Latta

"My Computer" (page 15) is used by permission of Peter Dabbene

"Truth, Justice and the American Way" (page 17) is used by permission of Angela Brinker

"Time" (page 19) is used by permission of Luigi Masella

"Brooklyn/LA" (page 20) is used by permission of John M. Alexander ©John M. Alexander

"Old Thermostat" (page 21) is used by permission of Stacie Younger

"Promises and Resolutions" (page 23) is used by permission of Elizabeth S. Hurowitz (www.elizabethsarah.com)

"Dog vs. Rabbit" (page 25) is used by permission of John Mikoley

"TV Family" (page 26) is used by permission of Christopher Herwig (www.herwigphoto.com)

"Lightning in a Bottle" (page 29) is used by permission of Kirsten Pauli

"Sex on the Beach" (page 31) is used by permission of Silvia Haniger

"Amber Amulet With Insect" (page 33) is used by permission of Jiahao Chen

"Strange Circle at Mountain View" (page 35) is used by permission of John J. Glenn (Crowolf Design)

"Forgotten" (page 37) is used by permission of Andrea de Poda

"Serious Calculations" (page 38) is used by permission of Erin Drewitz

"The Morning After the Night Before" (page 39) is used by permission of Tim Kirman

"First Car" (page 41) is used by permission of Peter Dabbene

"Street Light" (page 43) is used by permission of Colin Stevenson (www.colinstevenson.com)

"Thumper" (page 45) is used by permission of Anthony Smallwood

"Shh the Dead Are Sleeping" (page 47) is used by permission of Heather Shade (www.heathershade.com)

"The Space in Between" (page 49) is used by permission of Mark Hood (www.markhood.net)

"Grassy Field" (page 51) is used by permission of Michelle Bechard-Toth

"Annulment Begins" (page 53) is used by permission of Amanda Jansen

"Passed the Ball" (page 55) is used by permission of Robert Dowell

"Shhhhh" (page 57) is used by permission of Fernando de Sousa

"December Moon" (page 59) is used by permission of Ben Jeffries (benology101@yahoo.com)

"Open Book" (page 60) is used by permission of Brett Holt

"Snake" (page 63) is used by permission of Ben Jeffries (benology101@yahoo.com)

"Stonehenge is Closed" (page 65) is used by permission of Alastair McKay

"Reflective" (page 67) is used by permission of George E. Brown (www.georgebrownphotography.com)

"Wonder to See" (page 69) is used by permission of George E. Brown (www.georgebrownphotography.com)

"Solitude" (page 71) is used by permission of Érinn Cunningham (www.urbannation.net)

"Liberty" (page 73) is used by permission of George E. Brown (www.georgebrownphotography.com)

"Springing Forth in a California Sort of Way" (page 74) is used by permission of Jan Richards

"Philip Glass, Monumenta 2008" (page 77) is used by permission of Francois Bouchet

"Hale-Bopp 1" (page 79) is used by permission of Bernard Surette

"Dog Enjoying the View" (page 81) is used by permission of Mike Griggs (www.creativebloke.com)

"First Look" (page 83) is used by permission of Peter Dabbene

"Tree Reflected on Water No. 3743" (page 84) is used by permission of Sebastian Cowden

"Teething" (page 85) is used by permission of Sami Merriman

"What Are You Looking At?" (page 87) is used by permission of Peter Dabbene

"Beach Boy" (page 89) is used by permission of Peter Dabbene

"Second Glances" (page 90) is used by permission of Peter Dabbene

"The Whale, 2:30 a.m." (page 91) is used by permission of Peter Dabbene

"Crazy Guy in Times Square" (page 92) is used by permission of Dan Dickheiser

"The Glass is Always Half-Full" (back cover image) is used by permission of Scott Cahill Rude

ABOUT THE AUTHOR

Peter Dabbene looks like this:

Peter Dabbene lives in Hamilton, New Jersey. He was born in 1973. In addition to poetry, he has published two story collections, *Prime Movements* and *Glossolalia*, as well as a novel, *Mister Dreyfus' Demons*. Some of his stories can be found online at www.parentheticalnote.com, www.eyeshot.net, www.quantummuse.com, www.yankeepotroast.org, and www.wordriot.org, in print in *US 1*, *American Drivel Review*, *North Atlantic Review*, *Universe Pathways*, *Riversedge*, *Writer's Post Journal*, *Cantaraville*, in the music anthology *Tribute to Orpheus* and recorded in the audiozine *Scyweb Bem*. He has also reviewed books for *The Hamilton Post* and *The Ewing Observer* newspapers. He is currently writing a graphic novel called *Ark*, illustrated by Ryan Bayliss, which will be published in 2010.

Peter's website is www.peterdabbene.com

These poems were written from 2004-2007.

Optimist or pessimist? "I see the glass as having some water in it."

www.ingramcontent.com/pod-product-compliance
Lightning Source LLC
Chambersburg PA
CBHW040905020526
44114CB00037B/66